Ten Things About

Marriage
&
How to Create a
Godly One

Ten Things About

Marriage
&
How to Create a
Godly One

Reggie Weems

Unless otherwise noted, Scripture quotations are taken from The Holy Bible, English Standard Version® (ESV®) Copyright © 2001 by Crossway, a publishing ministry of Good News Publishers. All rights reserved. ESV Text Edition: 2016

Copyright © 2018, Reggie Weems
www.10thingsabout.org

All rights reserved. No part of this book may be reproduced, scanned, or distributed in any printed or electronic form without permission.

First Edition: 2018

ISBN 978-0-9996559-3-1

To buy quantities of this book at a special rate for bulk use, email
info@greatwriting.org

Great Writing Publications
www.greatwriting.org
Taylors, SC

Table of Contents

About the Series and this Book 9

Introduction 11

1 Before You Begin 15

2 The Meaning of Marriage 23

3 An Outpost of Heaven 31

4 An Evangelistic Enterprise 37

5 Ten Things 47

6 Conclusion 85

About the Author 89

Resources 90

For Tom

About the Series and this Book

TEN THINGS is a series of books offering biblical encouragement and practical direction on matters of concern to modern Christians who are seeking Bible-saturated, Christ-centered, Spirit-empowered, practical guidance. The series is published in an electronic and print format for quick, private, and easy access.

The books are brief and to the point, enabling readers to access immediate help and genuine hope for real-life situations. They are also written in a pastoral tone intended to shepherd hearts and minds toward Christ-centered, whole-life transformation.

This encouragement is not intended to and cannot replace personal pastoral counsel or the accountability of living transparently in Christian fellowship with other believers. Both are invaluable to you. A particular book may inspire a reader, but lifelong change only occurs in the context of living in biblical community.

Because of its biblical and simple approach, pastors may also employ the series to disciple church leaders who minister to God's flock.

Introduction

As a young, newly married couple, my wife and I were privileged to attend Grace Independent Baptist Church in Crownsville, Maryland. Tom Hawkins, to whom this book is dedicated, was the first pastor I ever knew and he was an exemplary model of personal, incarnational, enduring, pastoral ministry (Tom was the minister of that single congregation for twenty-five years). God called me to preach at a mission conference in that church, forever changing the direction of my life. Tom visited in our home to help me better understand that commitment. Thirty-eight years distant I remember his advice, and his pastoral paradigm still influences my ministry.

Tom also led our Sunday school class, held in his home next door to the church facility. I'm not much of a breakfast person so I can remember days when my stomach growled out loud, but the embarrassment has been replaced by laughter. That Sunday school class was also my initial experience with the powerful effect of small groups, a passion of Tom's and, ever since, of mine as well.

There is something else of particular importance that I remember about that congregation. Several weeks into our relationship with its membership, a couple invited us to Sunday lunch with their family. Just before we ate, the husband led all of us in prayer. After the meal, he and I cleaned the kitchen. In the afternoon, my wife and I watched them play with their children and put them to bed for naps. Throughout the day, the young husband and I enjoyed fellowship, as did our wives. Later in the afternoon, all four of us talked about life and marriage.

We lived there for less than six months but the Sunday lunch scenario continued until I left the military and our family, now including a new daughter, moved from Maryland. It was an enjoyable relationship. I only assume their kindness was an extension and reflection of the influence of Tom and his wife, Nancy. (Tom developed Multiple Sclerosis in 1986 and Nancy served as his full-time caregiver until Alzheimer's made it impossible for her to continue caring for him. Nancy met Jesus face to face in 2016, making all of us long all the more for heaven.)

My wife and I were not only a young married couple at that time but young Christians as well. Only years later did we realize that this family extended friendship to us with a discipling purpose—to model Christian marriage and to influence our marriage. We are eternally grateful to them and believe that heaven will reintroduce us so that we can properly thank them. But until then, I hope this book will in some small way repay the inestimable debt owed to this very influential pastor, church, and couple.

THINK ABOUT IT

The cross demonstrates the love that is foundational to a godly marriage and also provides the power to live that life.

1

Before You Begin:
A Word of Caution

You may have never previously considered marriage from a Christian perspective. If not, the biblical principles discussed in this book may initially appear startling. I assure you they are no different from Christ's call upon the whole of your life. One of the reasons the normal Christian life to which Jesus calls you may at first appear supranormal is because twenty-first-century Western Christianity has committed at least two ills: we have made Christianity all about us and, disconnected from the history of our faith, we think that's the way it ought to be. As a result, multitudes of sincere believers don't understand the "fullness of joy" (Psalm 16:11) of living holistically with a Christ-centered worldview as the basis for all of life, including—and especially—marriage.

Make no mistake about it, there is no other Jesus than the one who said to all, "If anyone would come after me, let him deny himself and take up his cross daily and follow me" (Luke 9:23).

Please remember that no one in history or Scripture ever carried a cross solely as an instrument of burden. A person didn't carry it for three miles as a temporary punishment, only to find eventual release from its weight. Jesus' meaning is crystal clear, as his own crucifixion demonstrated. Carrying a cross meant death.

Note that this verse…

1. is spoken to "all" potential Jesus-followers,
2. implies by "if" that you should count the cost,
3. demands the denial of self,
4. requires cross-bearing to "follow me," and
5. is a "daily," death-to-life experience.

Each of these sacrificial requirements is heightened by marriage vows and married life. Jesus' love for the church creates the basis for and meaning of marriage. It reflects a "greater" love (John 15:13) that dies to self for Someone (Jesus) and someone else (your spouse) only to discover abundant life and divine love on the other side of the temporary grave. In this, Jesus is our model, motivation, and means to live godly married lives. Viewed in its proper context, the idea of marriage should make us seriously reflect on our lives as Christians.

Marriage is an incredible gift from God—the most personally joyful, satisfying, and rewarding relationship on earth. But its inestimable value and incalculable reward are commensurate with the effort and, often, the difficulty required to ensure its success. Don't get me wrong. There is duty in marriage but it is, to rephrase John Piper, "a delightful duty." In other words, it is both a duty and a delight: a delightful duty and a dutiful delight; one that knows no greater joys or sorrows—and most of the sorrows are caused by our own sin.

Whenever I speak like this about marriage to engaged couples or to the adults in our congregation, my wife worries that I am discouraging young couples from marriage, or that I am representing marriage—especially ours—as the burden of a cross. I hope not. That is exactly the opposite of what I intend.

Our marriage is the most honest, joyful, rewarding relationship we possess on earth. And the other, most wonderful relationships we possess all emanate from it in our children, their spouses, and our grandchildren. She and I met as children, married very young, and our marriage only "gets better" every year. But its joy and satisfaction have multiplied beyond imagination by laying down our own lives, individually and as a couple, and taking up God's purposes for our marriage.

Again, a cross in Jesus' world was not an instrument of burden but of death. And on the other side of his death, Jesus was resurrected in the power of the Spirit and exalted to the Father's right hand. In the process, he gained a bride for himself and innumerable children for the Father. His suffering was temporary; his gain is eternal.

In like manner, marriage is God's call to a sanctifying relationship and any sanctification, while painful, is worth God's anvil. "For the moment all discipline seems painful rather than pleasant, but later it yields the peaceful fruit of righteousness to those who have been trained by it" (Hebrews 12:11). At the same time, the resurrected Christ provides the power and ability to live the life he modeled and requires of you.

Marriage is an incredible training ground for righteousness, in part because it is 24/7 and there is no place in it to hide your sin or your sinfulness. It is easier for you to be an unsaved church member or hypocritical Christian in church, work or social settings; marriage reveals the true you. The pain of that reality will either move you to repentance or anger. But the problem is not your spouse or your situation; it is that marriage reveals the true you and that is in itself a painful experience. But, if you will die to your self and its sin, you will discover a life that is available only through Christ's omnipotent grace.

I want to encourage you to make the time to prayerfully reflect on the married life God calls you to and repent of any misalignment. Then implement God's kingdom purposes in your marriage. Of course, all of this occurs by the Holy Spirit's power. If you do, Jesus' resurrected, enthroned life will enable you to live as a Christian husband, wife, and couple. As a result, the incredible "mystery" (Ephesians 5:32) of marriage will be revealed in you. The first step, trusting God alone, may be the hardest. But every step thereafter will be divinely enabled.

Action Points

1. How does self-centeredness ruin marriage?

_____

_____

_____

2. What model did Jesus present as the master plan for marriage?

_____

_____

3. Why is marriage a sanctifying environment?

_____

_____

4. How does Jesus' cross and resurrection provide power for marriage?

_____

_____

2

The Meaning of Marriage

Christian marriage is a holy, sanctifying relationship. It is also the most unique relationship on earth. No one should enter its union without seriously considering its spiritual requirements and potential blessings. Those requirements and blessings originate in God himself, his word, and his will. Marriage vows are not made only before a preacher or a congregation but also before God. He instituted holy matrimony and he requires that the promises you make at the altar of marriage shall be made real by actual, daily living.

This should impress on you the sacredness of marriage. The Father began this union between a man and a woman in Eden when he made Eve out of Adam and "brought her to the man" (Genesis 2:22). The Lord Jesus also honored the institution of marriage when he attended the wedding at Cana and performed his first miracle to ensure the ceremony's joyful success (John 2). The Holy Spirit taught the glory of marriage when he inspired the apostle Paul to compare the relationship between Jesus and his church to that of a husband and wife (Ephesians 5).

According to Romans 8:19-23, Christianity serves as a microcosm and preview of God's cosmic redemptive agenda. As a man and woman biblically love each other, marriage uniquely and publicly displays this creation-wide reconciliation agenda (Colossians 1:15-20). Marriage is also the primary medium by which God expands his kingdom (Genesis 12:3).

In Malachi 2, the prophet asked the priests of Israel about God's goal in marriage. What is "God seeking" (v. 15) in the covenant of marriage, he asks? "Godly offspring," he replies, answering his own question. This, according to Malachi, is one of the reasons for marriage and for guarding the intimacy of a marriage. Marriage is the means by which God fills the whole earth with the knowledge of himself (Genesis 1:28).

It is impossible to calculate the value of marriage. It is the means by which…

1. God reflects his love for the church,
2. demonstrates the joy of his salvation,
3. promotes his divine agenda,
4. provides a window into kingdom life here and now, and
5. previews the world to come.

Your marriage can reflect each of these elements. It all starts with a biblical vision of God's purpose for marriage.

Proverbs 29:18 reads: "Where there is no prophetic vision the people cast off restraint, but blessed is he who keeps the law." The word "restraint" means to "draw away from" or to "go loose" because of neglect and, in this particular verse, because people neglect the clear prophetic vision of God's law. As Adam and Eve demonstrated, without a clear vision of God's law, people tend to draw away from the Lord. This neglect always produces negative consequences. What you need is a clear "prophetic vision" of God's law concerning marriage. This will ensure God's blessings on your marriage; i.e., that you will inherit all God intends for you as a spouse and, perhaps, father or mother.

God's vision for marriage is the demonstration of Christ's sacrificial love for the church. Marriage is first about God's redemptive scheme working in and through you. God eternally saves you from his wrath by the cross and then daily saves you in the marriage relationship. It calls you to live like Jesus. This vision gives dignity, meaning, significance, direction, purpose, power, and hope to your marriage. Unless you realize this, your marriage will exist in constant controversy as you strive to center all things on you and your interpretation of marriage.

In the big picture of God's work in our world, God is moving all things from separation to reconciliation, from a fallen creation to the new creation. Insofar as marriage is concerned, alignment to God's cosmic purposes results in personal integrity and marital harmony. It also distinguishes your marriage from secular marriages. Living on mission with God draws a husband and wife closer together and focuses marriage and childrearing on God's kingdom work in each member of the family and then in the world. Fulfilling God's design will give your marriage a unique platform for gospel witness and influence. God's way is always the best way. Obedience possesses inherent blessings. You can have an incredible marriage if you are willing to commit yourself to God's mandate for marriage.

After salvation, marriage is perhaps the greatest experience of your life. And yet many people spend more time investing in the wedding ceremony or the honeymoon than they do in the marriage itself. If you consider how long the ceremony or the honeymoon will last in comparison to how long you hope your marriage will last, you will realize that many people have misguided priorities when planning for a lifetime of marriage. This is one reason why it is imperative that you seek marital counseling before you are married. Once married, it is also important for you to remain open to counseling, either in the friendship of couples who mentor you or professional counseling.

Living on mission with God is to live meaningfully, wholeheartedly, and fully. Take some time now to contemplate the spiritual requirements and real-life blessings of a biblical marriage founded on God's word and purposes. I hope that it will cause serious reflection, repentance where necessary, and productive conversation between you and your fiancé or you and your spouse.

Action Points

1. Explain how the Father, Son, and Holy Spirit make marriage a sacred relationship.

_____

_____

_____

2. How does marriage display God's reconciling love?

_____

_____

3. What is God's vision for marriage?

_____

_____

_____

4. How does marriage visualize the gospel to a world that is blind to it?

_____

_____

_____

3

Your Marriage as an
Outpost of Heaven

When the apostle Paul wrote to the Philippian church he encouraged them to live as "citizens of heaven…" (Philippians 3:20). This was an important concept for the recipients of this letter. The Philippi that Paul knew was conquered by Phillip II of Macedon in 356 BC. In an effort to control its area gold mines, Phillip established a garrison and enhanced the trade route that flowed through the city. The endeavor proved so successful that Philip eventually established a royal mint in Philippi, making it an important city for the eastern expansion of his kingdom.

The Romans gained control of the city in 166 BC. One hundred and twenty-four years later, Mark Antony and Octavian confronted and defeated several of the assassins of Julius Caesar at Philippi. To celebrate, they allowed veteran soldiers to retire there and colonize the city as an outpost of Rome. When Octavian became the Roman emperor (27 BC), he retired soldiers from the legendary Praetorian

Guard in Philippi. This made the city very loyal to Caesar, serving his interests and as a model of Rome itself on the empire's eastern border.

Paul's encouragement for the Romans to live as "citizens of heaven" asked them to value their Christian citizenship above that of Rome. This was a breathtakingly bold request. The Philippian church was undoubtedly comprised of some soldiers who had won their retirement at the risk of their lives. Living in Philippi as a free person was the kind of reward for which every Roman solider served in the military. The city and the church were very proud of their Roman heritage and representation of Rome. Paul's request to prize God's kingdom above that of Rome had gargantuan implications, and the Philippians fully understood Paul's meaning.

To live as a Christian in Philippi meant valuing God's kingdom principles above those of Rome. That empire existed as an honor-shame culture in which victory by conquest and the might-is-right mentality were honored. Strength was one of its highest values and servitude was deemed to be a shame. Of course, God's kingdom inverts that reality. It is a realm whose version of Octavian is a crucified Savior. It is a world in which the strong are commanded to view their strength as God's gift to serve his world. In

Christianity, leadership is always servant-hearted.

In his efforts to win the Philippians to a Christian worldview, Paul presented Jesus, Timothy, Epaphroditus, and himself as kingdom models (2:5-8, 19-30; 4:1-11). After listing his impressive credentials, the apostle wrote "whatever gain I had, I counted as loss for the sake of Christ" (3:7). He concluded his appeal with the words "Let those of us who are mature think this way…" (3:15) and "Brothers, join in imitating me, and keep your eyes on those who walk according to the example you have in us" (3:17). He then contrasted two ways of living, one to destruction by glorying in the wrong things (3:19); the other of living as citizens of heaven and participating in the eventual, cosmic, comprehensive victory of Jesus (20-21).

God intends your marriage to fulfill Paul's request to the Philippians. Your marriage is an outpost of heaven exhibiting new-world principles and practices. It is not supposed to represent the desires of a fallen, failing world (1 John 2:17) but instead to demonstrate the wonder and wellness of God's kingdom principles. Your marriage points forward to a life and world "without spot or blemish" (Ephesians 5:27) in which Jesus reigns. The world should look at your marriage and exclaim, "So this is love." This means that your marriage is counter-cultural to the world's preoccupation with the dominant and dominating self. But that difference will make it shine as a light in darkness, a city set on a hill (Matthew 5:14). And its influence is in its difference.

For a very general example, think about how you celebrate Easter and Christmas versus how the world celebrates these holydays. But it is not just in twice-a-year, large events. It is every minute of every day living that makes your marriage a Christian marriage. It is the meaning of your marriage and its purpose, the way you treat and speak to and about your spouse, the dignity with which you hold marriage and your spouse in esteem, the way you serve one another, the reason for having children, and the hope you have for them. All of these elements serve as pointers to remind you of God's kingdom and to guide others to it.

Action Points

1. How can a Christian marriage demonstrate "new world principles and practices"?

_____

_____

2. What particular virtues should be true of a Christian marriage?

_____

_____

3. What lifestyle did Jesus, Paul, Timothy, and Epaphroditus exhibit? How does that blueprint make Christian marriage unique?

_____

_____

4

Your Marriage as an Evangelistic Enterprise

Your Christian marriage will not look like the marriage of an unregenerate friend. Non-Christian marriages often begin and end with self. Your marriage begins with God and encompasses the entire globe.

The world has misinterpreted the meaning and purpose of marriage, making it another stepping stone to personal satisfaction at all costs. Non-Christians marry with personal pleasure as their highest priority. Christians also marry selfishly. Like the world, we marry people who make us happy. But by his Spirit, God transforms our self-centeredness into others-centeredness, mirroring Christ's servant-minded and sacrificial heart. Timothy, Epaphroditus, and Paul weren't the only models Paul presented in Philippians.

The apostle's greatest model for kingdom living is Jesus, of whom, Timothy, Epaphroditus, Paul, and we are simply reflections. Think about how these verses apply to the most intimate human relationship you possess, that of husband and wife. Then contemplate how the application of these verses could radically alter your marriage relationship and provide a platform for sharing the gospel in a world that endures the opposite of what Paul is encouraging. The apostle writes:

> So if there is any encouragement in Christ, any comfort from love, any participation in the Spirit, any affection and sympathy, complete my joy by being of the same mind, having the same love, being in full accord and of one mind. Do nothing from selfish ambition or conceit, but in humility count others more significant than yourselves. Let each of you look not only to his own interests, but also to the interests of others. Have this mind among yourselves, which is yours in Christ Jesus, who, though he was in the form of God, did not count equality with God a thing to be grasped, but emptied himself, by taking the form of a servant, being born in the likeness of men. And being found in human form, he humbled himself by becoming obedient to the point of death, even death on a cross. (2:1-8).

According to Paul, the Holy Spirit produces affection, sympathy, joy, love, and like-mindedness—all strategically laser focused into the sacrificial life modeled by Jesus himself. The selfless humility of preferring others to self, as demonstrated by Jesus, is everything the Roman empire and its citizens attempted to avoid. Such an appeal certainly made Paul's Roman readers nervous. But much to their delight, he didn't finish his appeal with Jesus on the cross. Jesus' death and life possess eternal consequences from which the Philippians benefited as they repented of sin and trusted Christ as Savior. Paul continued:

> Therefore God has highly exalted him and bestowed on him the name that is above every name, so that at the name of Jesus every knee should bow, in heaven and on earth and under the earth, and every tongue confess that Jesus Christ is Lord, to the glory of God the Father. (2:9-11).

In Paul's theology, the cross won Jesus eternal glory. It also won him a bride. Your marriage is intended to win you wholly to Christ, your spouse as well, your children also. In so doing, it evangelizes the lost, making others jealous to know the God who gives you and your family such relational peace and overflowing joy.

In Christianity, the way up is down, the way to life is death, and the way to fullness is emptying oneself. The way to gain life is to give life (Luke 9:24). Giving your life away to your spouse and/or children will gain you the life you truly want. It will also present a natural platform for displaying the good news of God's grace.

Giving his life away, Jesus gained an exalted life to be eventually enjoyed with his redeemed family. This is what it cost Jesus to wed himself to the church. This is the life God calls you to in marriage. This is how you live "blameless and innocent, children of God without blemish in the midst of a crooked and twisted generation, among whom you shine as lights in the world, holding fast to the word of life…" (2:15-16a).

Don't miss that important point: a godly life, and in this context, your godly marriage, is a light to the world, reflecting Jesus' love and pointing people to God. This is how your marriage changes you and transforms the people around you. The way to a happy marriage is holiness—obedience to God's word, living as ambassadors of Christ's love. In effect, marriage is God's olive branch to the world. Your marriage says, "This is how Jesus loves. Come and experience his love." As such, every Christian marriage should be and can be an evangelistic witness to the world.

Paul's request for the Roman Christians of Philippi could cost the Philippians everything—but not really. It actually promised them everything: everything only omniscience and omnipotence can provide. It's your daily decision: the life God gives or the life you can create; omnipotence or finiteness.

If you are planning to be married or if you are already married and desire to have a godly marriage, here are ten important things to know about marriage as God created and intends it—what it will cost you and what it will give you. But first, let's think about what we've already discussed.

Action Points

1. In his incarnation, Jesus' mind was set on humility and servanthood. What would your marriage look like if these were the foundational stones to your attitude and actions?

_____

_____

2. Consider another Christian couple whom your marriage could influence. How might you accomplish this? Invite them to a meal, to spend a day with you, etc?

_____

_____

3. How could you, as a couple, intentionally influence an unsaved couple toward Christ? (I'm not suggesting this as an evangelistic strategy or church program. That would be shallow, unfulfilling, and ineffective. I am

saying that God's love naturally overflows into a shared experience.)

_____

_____

_____

You could begin by praying together for them. You could invite them to a meal or to an event with your family, perhaps to your Thanksgiving or Christmas meal. The potential opportunities are virtually limitless. It's simply a matter of seeing your marriage as God's means to expand his kingdom.

To help you better understand the meaning of marriage and God's life-changing purposes for it, the next chapter provides ten things to help you create and maintain a godly marriage.

THINK ABOUT IT

Trinitarian love overflows into the creation of everything that exists. Godly, married love overflows into the lives of others.

5

Ten Things about
Creating a Godly Marriage

You've been waiting for this list. We love lists. Few things make us feel better about ourselves—capable, effective, successful and validated—than checking things off of a list. But you should be careful with this list.

Don't mistake reading this list or knowing these things for godliness or life transformation. We are changed only as the Holy Spirit applies God's truth to our lives. Pray that God will do just that.

Before you read, pray for enlightenment and the spirit of repentance. You don't have to read the whole list in one sitting. You could consider taking ten days to read each point each day, asking God to make his truth come alive in you. This book has no power. Only God has power (Psalm 62:1; Romans 1:16). It can, however, create the environment of space and time for God to work his truth deep into your soul and for the Holy Spirit to apply this truth. Time plus truth equals transformation. Take the time and make the effort to read deeply for a bountiful harvest.

Repent where needed. (Repentance is a change of mind and heart that results in changed behavior.) Thereafter (and for the rest of your life) keep a short sin-list, living as a repenter.

Ensure your spouse reads the book. It is important for a husband and wife to grow together. Learn the same principles and apply the same truths. Determine together to live as a godly couple committed to God's redemptive agenda in you and in the world.

And give yourselves time. You will succeed and fail. You will disappoint your spouse and yourself. But God's grace is sufficient. In the interim, trust God for what he alone can do as you "work out your own salvation with fear and trembling, for it is God who works in you, both to will and to work for his good pleasure" (Philippians 2:12-13).

ONE

As the home goes, so goes the world.

The maxim "As the home goes, so goes the world" is very true. Marriage is the first institution God ever created. As such, it forms the foundation for all other human institutions. This means that every Christian marriage potentially affects the entire world. The home of today creates the world of tomorrow. It is the template for human harmony or conflict. It presents either the gospel as the only hope of the world or it presents a contradictory message. This makes marriage an incredible privilege and a daunting responsibility.

Consider the model of our first parents. When Adam and Eve sinned, their marital rebellion thrust all creation into chaos (Romans 8:20). Now, all creation looks toward humanity as the hope and model for renewal (Romans 8:23).

Nothing that happens in your home remains inside its four walls. There is no degree of separation between your home and the world. Every virtue and every vice you display eventually influences the rest of the world for good or bad. You are daily influencing the world one way or another. This makes your every attitude and action in marriage exponentially and universally important. It makes your marriage pivotal to God's redemptive scheme.

Your marriage and home can enjoy the fruit of the Spirit—love, joy, peace, patience, kindness, goodness, faithfulness, gentleness, self-control (Galatians 5:22-23)—or it can endure the "works of the flesh… sexual immorality, impurity, sensuality, idolatry, sorcery, enmity, strife, jealousy, fits of anger, rivalries, dissensions, divisions, envy, drunkenness and orgies…" (Galatians 5:20-21). But make no mistake about it. Your marriage can exhibit and enjoy intentional godliness as you and your spouse (and children if you have them) live out the principles God's kingdom, producing *shalom* first in your family and then in the world. Or your married life will spell d-i-s-a-s-t-e-r for you and the world. The seeds for global joy or sorrow tomorrow are planted today in your marital relationship. Incredibly, your marriage is a pivotal key to the world's joy or sorrow, success or failure.

As you consider this reality, and everything else said in this book, remember that the gospel is your personal and marital salvation. God will complete the work he has begun in you (Philippians 1:6). He will grant you the desire and ability to do his will (Philippians 2:13). He will even take your past or present failures and turn them for your good and the good of those you love (Romans 8:28). It is your privilege to participate in God's redemptive drama in the world. But the responsibility for its fulfillment belongs to God. He alone can and will bring all things to their intended end. The gospel is a declaration of God's accomplished victory, not your continuing efforts. Be a gospel-responsible husband or wife. Live in the Spirit. But don't assume God's responsibility. This balance makes the gospel good news.

After all, as the home goes, so goes the world.

TWO

The Trinity provides the blueprint for marriage.

God's eternal community provides the blueprint for marriage. It reflects the fellowship in which God eternally dwells. Soon after God created Adam and placed him in the garden, he gave him the privilege of naming every animal. Just before naming the animals the Scripture reads, "Then the LORD God said, 'It is not good that the man should be alone; I will make him a helper fit for him.'" The very next two verses detail the naming of the animals and the occasion ends with the haunting words, "But for Adam there was not found a helper fit for him" (Genesis 2:18-20).

God knew it was not good for Adam to live alone but prior to naming the animals Adam didn't understand the concept of aloneness. Naming the animals—undoubtedly one pair after another—demonstrated aloneness to Adam. That's why God said it was not good for Adam to be alone, had him name the animals, and immediately afterward created Eve, whom he then "brought" to Adam (Genesis 2:22). Only after naming the animals did Adam understand what it meant to be alone. Only after Eve's creation did he know what it meant not to be alone. By creating Adam first, having him name the animals and then creating Eve, God "storied" his desire for humanity.

Our God is one God revealed in three persons. He lives in a forever community. Adam and Eve each bear God's image and were created to live together in community. Marriage represents the fundamental nature of our Trinitarian God in a multitude of ways. I'm not suggesting that the members of the Trinity correlate to the members of a family—God to a father, Jesus to a wife, and the Holy Spirit to children. But I am saying that God naturally lives in eternal community and marriage reflects the intimacy of the plurality and unity of that divine community.

Marriage and family present the first community that all human beings experience. It is intended to model and function in relational alignment with God's triune existence and mission. This is where husbands, wives, and children learn to live relationally healthy or sick lives. And that experience determines how we relate to others outside of the family, creating a template for how the world relates to itself.

THREE

Marriage is a mirror of redemption with Jesus as the ultimate groom.

God's point in the naming exercise was not simply to prove to Adam that he was alone. The account doesn't end there. The next verses (Genesis 2:21-23) detail Eve's creation, that God "brought her to the man," and that Adam understood Eve to be "bone of my bones and flesh of my flesh." Adam called Eve "woman, because she was taken out of man." Moses' comment in verse 24 defines the point of the narrative. He writes: "Therefore a man shall leave his father and his mother and hold fast to his wife, and they shall become one flesh."

In the creation of Eve, God removed Eve from Adam. Marriage reunites Adam and Eve and their descendants. It's a wonderful picture of reconciliation. Just as Christ, a groom, moves toward a bridge and marriage, so Christ has come to us. The marriage of Adam and Eve also resulted in banishment from the Garden and the fall of creation. And redemption results in the reuniting of all things to

God. God intends your marriage to be a living demonstration of his work "to reconcile to himself all things" (Colossians 1:20). Your marriage makes you and your spouse "one flesh" (Genesis 2:24; Matthew 19:5-6). Marriage is a mirror of redemption and Jesus is the ultimate groom.

This is why divorce is so traumatic. It is the tearing of that "one flesh" principle. The negative effects of divorce are clearly visible. You have undoubtedly witnessed the heartbreaking sorrow involved in the dissolution of a marriage. But the greatest cost is invisible and incalculable. Innumerable people are walking around with torn flesh, i.e., ripped emotions, divided minds, etc. You have seen it. Perhaps you have endured it. Marriage teaches us how to relate as the Trinity relates, in love and unity. Divorce leaves people in isolation and with unresolved relational conflict. Both marriage and divorce affect the whole of your life and especially relationships. This is why marriage and divorce are such significant matters. Marriage reflects God's reconciling work in the world. Divorce represents the undoing of what God is doing.

FOUR

Biblical marriage is the environment for God to create a people for himself.

The Trinitarian nature of God also defines biblical marriage as the union of one man and one woman. There are at least two reasons why this is so. First, creation is the overflow of Trinitarian love. The love between a husband and wife also overflows into the creation of others. Only the union of a man and woman can accomplish this reproduction.

Second, before the foundation of the world God planned to create a people for himself. For that reason, the Father planned our salvation (Ephesians 1:4), the Son purchased our salvation (1:7), and the Holy Spirit protects our salvation (1:13). This could not have happened if our God did not exist as one God in three distinct persons. For instance, the Son, and not the Father, died at Calvary. The Father, not the Son, remained in heaven during the incarnation. The Spirit, not the Father or Son, fell upon believers in the Upper Room at Pentecost. The Father, Son, and Holy Spirit, as one God, yet distinct persons, are essential for creation and redemption. Marriage only reflects the Trinity if the husband and wife are one flesh but are not the same, each a distinct person and who together are able, by that distinction, to model God's redemptive agenda in the world. Biblical marriage creates the environment in which God can continue this work of creating a people for himself.

Biblical marriage enables that mirror reflection of God's Trinitarian nature and purposes. It models redemption in the community of two different persons: God and sinners. Marriage is a reuniting of Adam and Eve, a man and a woman. This reflects the reuniting of Christ and humanity in salvation. It is a picture of Christ and his church.

God is not like humans. This makes salvation possible. Humans are not like God. This makes salvation necessary. Only the marriage of two distinct persons, a man and a woman, accurately reflects God's character and redemptive agenda. But the point of this point is to ensure you know that what God intends for your marriage—that it is to reflect his redemptive agenda in the world. You may or may not be able to have physical children. If you can, your own children are your first mission field. As a husband, you shepherd your own soul, that of your wife, and of your children. But if you do not have children, your marriage can produce spiritual children as you intentionally interact with unbelievers and introduce them to saving faith in Christ. You can also multiply your marriage in other marriages by investing in other couples.

FIVE

God gives husbands to wives to demonstrate God's love.

In Ephesians 5:25, Paul writes, "Husbands, love your wives…" In this passage, the apostle informs us that Christ's love for the church presents a model for marriage relationships and that marriage then reflects Christ's love for the church. We know this because Paul concludes this passage with the explanation, "This mystery is profound, and I am saying that it refers to Christ and his church" (5:32).

God planned marriage so that a husband could demonstrate God's love to a woman and so that woman could experience God's love from her husband. Children then learn the gospel by watching their parents. It is by a father's love for a mother that a son or daughter understand the nature and extent of God's love for them. This is how a son learns to love like God. This is how a daughter learns what it means to be loved. This is how a son learns to biblically love a wife. This is how a daughter learns how a husband should biblically love her. Christ's love for the church serves as the basis for marriage. It also provides marriage with a divine purpose—reflecting God's love for the church in the relationship between a husband and a wife.

Paul writes that husbands are to love their wives as "Christ loved the church and gave himself up for her." This ensures no husband has to wonder what God's love for his wife through him should look like. The Bible not only tells him what to do (love your wife), but it also tells him how to do it "and gave himself up for her." God loved us first (1 John 4:19). That love is the motivation and model for a husband's love for his wife. God's love is sacrificial (Romans 5:8). God's love serves (Mark 10:45). Life by death is a fundamental Christian principle of life and marriage. We die to self in order to live. We die to the world in order to live in a godly way. We demonstrate God's love by laying down our life for those we love (John 15:13). In response, God gives us what we most want: abundant and eternal life.

These are just a few of the ways that Jesus demonstrates his love for the church. This is how a husband should demonstrate his love for his wife. But this expression of sacrificial love should be the same in private and in public. In this way, a wife and the world get to see Jesus' love "with skin on."

SIX

Loving God is the reason for loving your wife.

You may be concerned that your wife might take advantage of such sacrificial love. But you don't love your wife so she will love you. You love your wife by and with God's love that you know, experience, and enjoy. Your love for her is an overflow of God's love for you just as creation is the overflow of Trinitarian love.

And you don't love your wife hoping in her response, but for God's pleasure. Your faith is not in your wife, it is in God. Don't let your ultimate hope be in her; that is idol worship. Trust in God who alone can give you both love for each other and transform your hearts.

As our model, God loved you long before you ever loved him—before you were ever created. You don't make yourself lovely for God to love to you. God's love makes you lovely. You can't merit, earn, and don't deserve God's love. God doesn't love you because you are lovely but because he is lovely.

In the same fashion, your love for your wife says more about you and your relationship to God than it does about your wife and your relationship to her.

This is love by grace and it's the way you are called to love your wife—as Christ loves the church. As previously mentioned, God loved you before the foundation of the world (Ephesians 1:4), long before you could have responded to his overtures. God's love for you is not dependent on your love for him. Nor should your love for your wife depend on her love for you. Instead, it is resourced by God's love for and in you.

Ephesians 2:4 informs us that the richness of God's mercy and the great love of God is the motive for salvation. In other words, God does not foresee your faith and save you on the basis of your response to his overtures. That would equate to a works-salvation. Likewise, you do not love your wife to the degree she loves you. Nor do you love her as she loves you, act for act, etc. No marriage can survive by keeping that kind of score. That is not the way God loves you and it is not the way you should love your wife. Your love should not be selfishly motivated. You should love your wife without demanding reciprocation.

Don't stop loving your wife even if she ceases to submit to you or you feel she is taking advantage of your love. In an effort to present her "in splendor without blemish sports or wrinkle...holy and without blemish" you will need to confront her about her selfishness. To do this, you must understand the difference between kindness and love.

Human kindness is often unwilling to make another person uncomfortable. Love is willing to make a person uncomfortable for that person's best interests. Kindness really thinks of self. Love thinks of the other person. Kindness may endure sin to avoid conflict. In that regard, kindness is self-preservation. Love will not tolerate sin. God is not simply kind to us. God loves us. For this reason, he confronts us as sinners and convicts us as Christians. In like manner, there are occasions when love for your wife will cause you to confront her about ungodly attitudes or actions.

A word of caution is appropriate at this point. In Ephesians 5:33 Paul encouraged a husband to "love his wife as himself, and [also to] let the wife see that she respects her husband." Based on this text you might infer that you, as a husband, should love your wife to gain her respect or that you, as a wife, should respect your husband to gain his love. But this application makes you a selfish person. You should love your wife for God's glory, your and her good. You should submit to your husband for God's glory, your and his good. You are not loving and submitting to *get* love and respect but to *give* love and respect. This reflects God's character. Again, to do otherwise is to make your wife or husband an idol, as though a spouse can satisfy your life with what only God possesses. Your ultimate trust is not in your husband or wife but in God. He is the cause and reward of your obedience.

Your love as a husband is based on the model of Christ's love for the church. Your response doesn't initiate God's love. God loved you when you were his enemy (Romans 5:10). His love is not dependent on you but himself. Nor is God's love maintained by your actions. It is solely dependent on the finished work of Jesus on the cross. You are called upon to love your wife in the like manner, mirroring Christ's love for you.

SEVEN

Jesus' submission to the Father models and elevates a wife's submission.

A godly wife will not take advantage of her husband's self-sacrificing love. Instead, the Scripture encourages wives to also demonstrate a particular aspect of Trinitarian love. Paul's counsel to wives in that passage is "Wives, submit to your own husbands, as to the Lord" (Ephesians 5:22) and he repeats that counsel in Colossians 3:18. There are at least two reasons for this.

First, "the husband is the head of the wife even as Christ is the head of the church, his body, and is himself its Savior." To demonstrate that biblical model of salvation, "wives should submit in everything to their husbands." This demonstrates the church's submission to Christ (5:24).

Second, a wife's submission also reflects the Son's submission to the Father. Again, this does not mean a wife "plays the part" of the Son in marriage. It does mean that the Father loves the Son and that is the context of the Son's submission. The Son's submission equally demonstrates a love for the Father. People in the modern era worry about the topic of submission because it has been abused by modern society. But submission is a biblical concept. Jesus is equal with the Father in the same way a woman is equal with a man—taken from his side and also made in God's image. Nevertheless, the Son submitted to the Father in the incarnation and passion (John 8:29). This makes the Son the divine model for submission. It also elevates the doctrine of submission within a marriage.

As a wife, you may be concerned that your husband will take advantage of such submission. Remember that your ultimate submission is to God and not your husband. Submission trusts God. By it, you are loving God. And your hope is not in your husband; that equates to idol worship. Your hope is in God.

Your submission is a response to God's love, not that of your husband. In submission, you are trusting God, not your husband. Do not make your husband an idol. You do not submit to gain the love of your husband. Your obedience is not motivated by your husband's love but motivated and resourced by Christ's love for and in you. He is your model of submission and he has given you his Spirit to replicate his willing, joyful submission which, for you, is first and ultimately to the Father.

In reality, everyone in a family submits to

someone. Husbands submit to Christ. Wives submit to husbands. Children submit to parents. Keep in mind that the submission and surrender despised by Rome is prized by God.

As a husband, you submit to God in loving your wife "as Christ loves the church" (Ephesians 5:25) and not leading/loving by your own design. Husbands submit themselves to God's love and lead by love. In other words, a loving husband leads in a biblical sense and an unloving husband does not biblically lead his wife or children. Paul qualifies a husband's love two ways: "as Christ loved the church" (v. 25) and "as their own bodies" (v. 28).

Wives also give evidence of their love for Christ and trust in God by submission. It is not ultimately about submitting to a husband but "to the Lord." In fact, you are to submit to your husband "as to the Lord" (5:22). This implies that your submission is guarded by righteousness and godliness; you can and should disobey if obedience to your husband causes you to disobey Christ. It also implies that your submission is really between you and God. In this way, you model the life of Christ in relationship to his Father. Similarly, your husband's love is not dependent on your response.

The end of this marital relationship is salvation. Husbands love and wives submit "that he [a husband] might sanctify her, having cleansed her by the washing of water with the word, so that he might present the church to himself in splendor, without spot or wrinkle or any such thing, that she might be holy and without blemish" (5:26-27).

EIGHT

Marriage requires putting off the old self and putting on the new self.

The great hope of marriage is that it will enjoy and reflect Christ's love for the church and the church's love for Jesus. This other-centered relationship will generate a never-ending cycle of love. But the kind of love God requires, love that never fails, (1 Corinthians 13:8) cannot be humanly generated. This requires God's love through you. But then again, that is why God created marriage—for you both to be ravished by God's love and the overflow of that love to shout the need for and the joy of the gospel to the world.

Colossians lays the foundation for Christian relationships as "compassionate, kind, humble, meek, patient, forbearing, forgiving, loving, harmonious, peaceful, and thankful" (Colossians 3:12-15). This is accomplished by choosing to "put to death" the unregenerate attitudes and actions of "sexual immorality, impurity, evil desire, covetousness, anger, wrath, malice, slander, obscenity and lying…"

(3:5-9). This is what it means to "put off the old self" and "put on the new self" (3:9-10). God calls you to exhibit these attitudes and actions in your marriage. The "new self" is a supernatural life that occurs as you "[l]et the word of Christ dwell in you richly…do[ing] everything in the name of the Lord Jesus" (3:16-17). The life (and in this situation, the marriage) you want is obtained by obeying the Father, enacting the model of Jesus in the power of the Spirit.

These are the qualities that you should value as a Christian and exhibit as a husband, wife, and parent. They are supernaturally produced in you as you actively, daily choose to die to yourself and live to God. This is a blueprint for personal and marital health. Each of these qualities deserves individual attention and study. These verses deserve to be memorized so that the Spirit of God can take the word of God and live Christ's life in you. Imagine having perfect love, compassion, patience, and kindness. Imagine being able to perfectly forgive. In this life, you will never be able to do these things perfectly. But as you set your mind on these kingdom values and you pray for God's grace to exhibit them, your life will be sufficiently transformed into the image of Jesus to create a holistically healthy life and marriage.

Notice, as well, that Paul's encouragement

begins with love and ends with peace. The end of God's love is peace between God and the church, a husband, wife, and children. In this way, Christian marriage practices and preaches the gospel of reconciliation for all the world to see and embrace.

NINE

Marriage is a preview of the new world to come.

Minus God's grace and your intentional commitment to a Christian marriage, old-world principles will surface in your relationship. God intends to reconcile all things to himself—and your married relationship is a demonstration of his power to do so—the new world to come. Satan, on the other hand, works to bring division in the world. One of his primary tactics is to destroy marriages.

Colossians 3:8-9 presents the divisive results of old-world living. If you are not careful, you will find that any disagreement between yourself and your spouse may grow into any of these terrible attitudes and actions. Paul lists them as individual sins but they may also be viewed as progressively harmful to your relationship. Consider this potential application of Paul's list (Colossians 3:8-9).

Anger toward a spouse says, "You have disappointed, not fulfilled me." If it is not repented of quickly, it can turn to wrath which cries, "You don't deserve my love and so I'm not talking to you." That silence creates an environment in which unprofitable thinking generates malice. It declares, "I am perpetually upset, so don't talk to me."

How do you expect your spouse to respond to such a statement? You are angry if your spouse does talk to you and angry if your spouse does not approach you. And after a period of silence, your heart and mind become so full of anger, wrath, and malice that you then slander your spouse with the words, "You never," or "You always." Both of these are, of course, untrue sentiments. No one "never" doesn't do anything or "always" does anything. "Obscene talk" doesn't necessarily mean cursing. It is any talk that is unfruitful. Paul condemned this kind of language in Ephesians 4:29. This unresolved conflict can lead one or both you lying to yourself and your spouse in the announcement, "I'm fine and can live without you." It is a downward spiral that can only be circumvented by constant obedience to God's word and, specifically, living as a repentant Christian.

Not one of those attitudes or actions listed in that text is a redemptive thought or behavior. They are not generated by love, nor do they create peace. Marriage is an environment intended to save us from our worst selves and demonstrate reconciliation to a watching world. It is also the environment in which the next generation learns to love God and others as a witness to his amazing, life-transforming grace.

Marriage represents that new world to come. It thrives on characteristics of harmony, unity and reconciliation. It is contrary to the old world with the divisive, damaging characteristics Paul listed in the Colossians 3 passage. Paul demonstrates this new world principle when he uses the word "regeneration" in Titus 3:5. It's the intentional use of the same Greek word Jesus used in Matthew 19:25 but there but translated "new world." What does Paul mean? He means that God's regeneration of you is the same work God is doing in the world. You are the template for and model of the new world. Your life and marriage is a picture of the new world to come. Your "regeneration" is the "new world" in principle and practice. You are the whole world God is creating wrapped up in one single person and one married couple. To put it another way, God is creating a whole world of regenerated people just like you. And as this old world passes away (1 John 2:17) you are the paradigm and picture for the new world to come.

TEN

**Loving children requires
hope in God,
not yourself or your children.**

If God graces your marriage with children, the Scripture provides a blueprint for those relationships. Colossians 3:18-31 speaks to the issues that face wives, husbands, children, and parents. Specifically, Paul's admonition offers counsel at the greatest family stressors: for husbands to love as Christ, wives to submit as Christ, and children to obey as Christ. It also demonstrates the purpose and hope of each respective role—to live as Christ.

According to these verses, it must be that loving without harshness is a husband's particular need. Submission must be difficult for wives. As those who have been children once ourselves, we can all agree that obedience is hard. If we are honest, we still suffer, even as adults, from that malady.

Hoping in God is the ultimate value for parents. We are to teach our children God's word (Deuteronomy 6:7). We are to model Christian virtues. We are to discipline our children for their own sakes (Ephesians 6:4). But behind, underneath, and beyond all our efforts as parents, we must hope in God. Only God can change a child's heart. Our task is really an impossible one. Our goal as parents is not simply to teach our children to obey but to want to obey. That is a work only God can accomplish.

The rationale for children obeying parents is to learn how to obey God. This is why you cannot surrender your parental responsibilities. Until your child leaves your home, you are preparing him or her for a lifetime of loving and obeying God. This is why you create rules, enact discipline, and reward obedience.

And it is all accomplished in the context of hoping in God; trusting him and not our parenting abilities or techniques; trusting him and not our children's positive or negative responses. Our hope for our children is not us or them but God.

THINK ABOUT IT

Marriage is the most sanctifying relationship on earth. Iron sharpening iron (Proverbs 27:17) will definitely create friction and sparks. It will also conform you into the image of Jesus.

Action Points

As you have seen, Ephesians 5:22-33 contains one of the most famous passages on marriage. The chapter begins with Paul's encouragement for his readers to "be imitators of God, as beloved children. And walk in love, as Christ loved us and gave himself up for us, a fragrant offering and sacrifice to God" (vv. 1-2).

Notice that Christ's loving sacrifice is both the model and the power for how Paul will later ask Ephesian husbands and wives to live. A husband's love and a wife's submission are Spirit-empowered imitations of the God who "emptied himself, by taking the form of a servant, being born in the likeness of men. And being found in human form, he humbled himself by becoming obedient to the point of death, even death on a cross" (Philippians 2:7-8). No other love story ever written can compare to the love of Jesus for his bride.

The greatest romance ever enacted transpired in Jesus' passion (death, burial, and resurrection). His life empowers your life as a husband and wife, providing you with the same passionate love story. It is yours in Christ.

Words to Wives

Think about what God is asking you to do: "Wives, submit to your own husbands…" (v. 22).

- Are you submitting to your husband?
  - ☐ Yes
  - ☐ No

If not, why not?

_____

_____

Think about the qualifier: "as to the Lord" (v. 22). Understand why God is commanding this:
"For the husband is the wife even as Christ is the head of the church, his body…" (v. 23).

- Do you see your husband in relation to

you as Christ is in relation to the church?
- ☐ Yes
- ☐ No

Look at the result of the church's submission: "and is himself its Savior" (v. 23).

▸ How might your submission "save" you?

_____

_____

Wives, then, should "submit in everything to their husbands" just "as the church submits to Christ" (v. 24).

This means God is not asking you to do anything (submit) he does not also require of your husband as a member of his church.

In addition, Jesus is your model of submission. Paul reminds us that Jesus "who for the joy that was set before him endured the cross, despising the shame, and is seated at the right hand of the throne of God" (Hebrews 12:2).

▸ Are you submitting to your husband as Christ did the Father and as your husband does the Lord? If not, why not?
- ☐ Yes
- ☐ No

- If not, why not?

_____

_____

- If your husband is not submitting to Christ, does that justify your disobedience?
  - ☐ Yes
  - ☐ No

Words to Husbands

Think about what God is asking you to do: "Husbands, love your wives…" (v. 25).

- How are you displaying love to your wife?

_____

_____

Consider and understand the qualifier: "as Christ loved the church and gave himself up for her" (v. 25).

- Is self-sacrifice an appropriate term to describe your love for your wife?
  - ☐ Yes
  - ☐ No

- Contemplate the purpose of your love:

"…that he might sanctify her, having cleansed her by the washing of the water with the word, so that he might present the church to himself in splendor, without spot or wrinkle or any such thing, that she might be holy and without blemish" (vv. 26-27).

- Is your love for your wife, sanctifying her?
  - ☐ Yes
  - ☐ No

- Do you understand that to love your wife is to love yourself (vv. 28-29)?
  - ☐ Yes
  - ☐ No

This love and submission relationship is the reason God created marriage (v. 31). In so living, a husband and wife make visible the mystery of Jesus' love for the church.

God has given a husband and wife the great privilege of imaging the love that exists between the Father, the Son, and the Holy Spirit. In addition, your love for each other demonstrates Christ's love for the church. As such, there is no higher honor than to be a husband and wife.

- Do you see your calling as a husband and wife to image (represent) God's love?
  - ☐ Yes
  - ☐ No

- How are you doing this?

  _____

  _____

- If you are not, what changes must be made for your marriage relationship to correctly represent God?

  _____

  _____

6

Conclusion

Marriage is God's Salvation Workshop

The great story of Jesus' love is told in the Gospels. But your love story has yet to be fully written. God has given you the gift of marriage to give and receive his saving love.

Marriage is God's divine workshop for modeling his cosmically comprehensive and personally holistic salvation. It demonstrates the love and joy of living in God's kingdom. It conforms us to the image Jesus. Creating a godly marriage possesses incredible rewards. But those blessings require hard work.

Marriage is not first about you but God and then others. Adam and Eve's selfishness illustrates the tragedy of self-centered living—a lesson sadly unlearned and tragically repeated in modern marriages. Everyone suffers from inherent self-centeredness. But God's rescue is all sufficient. The death of Jesus saves us once and for all from the wrath of God, and the life of Jesus continually saves us from ourselves (Romans 5:10).

In God's kingdom, you die to live and the

life God promises is more than you could ever create on your own. This makes marriage a uniquely rewarding relationship and simultaneously difficult. It is the most sanctifying environment and relationship on the planet. But the inherent value of a thing is often determined by the degree of difficulty required to obtain it. This is particularly true of marriage because it models Jesus and his amazing, relentless, victorious love for the church.

In marriage, your old nature will fight you. The world will conspire against you with the presentation of failing, mechanistic, self-help models. And Satan will provide ongoing temptations to devalue your vows, your spouse, yourself, and your God. But the Spirit of Jesus in you has and will continue to overcome the world, the flesh, and the devil, and give you a life and marriage beyond your own ability and imagination.

And remember, this book can never replace the incarnational ministry of living in community with others. You need a church home. You need pastoral ministry and the regular influence of the preached word. You also need to experience life (a) with, other couples who can inspire and instruct you, (b) who are equally committed to Christ, and (c) who need your inspiration and practical help. You need the balance of all three. They need you and you need them. Together, you will rejoice in God's salvation and reflect his love to the world.

About the Author

REGGIE WEEMS is married to his childhood sweetheart, Teana. They share three children and nine grandchildren. He has pastored two congregations: the first for ten years and the second since 1991. He also teaches theology, Bible, and humanities at two universities. His DMin in Pastoral Leadership and Management is from Liberty University, and his PhD in Historical Theology is from the University of Babes-Bolyai in Cluj-Napoca, Romania.

www.10thingsabout.org

To buy quantities of this book at a special rate for bulk use, email
info@greatwriting.org

Resources

I do want to offer you resources so that the word of Christ will continue to dwell richly in you as your marriage becomes all that God intends. But too many resources can be confusing. Here are just three that I think will be of great benefit to you.

This Momentary Marriage by John Piper

The Meaning of Marriage by Tim Keller

Shepherding a Child's Heart by Ted Tripp

www.ingramcontent.com/pod-product-compliance
Lightning Source LLC
Chambersburg PA
CBHW070547300426
44113CB00011B/1820